THE CALL OF THE
OSPREY

THE CALL OF THE
OSPREY

DOROTHY HINSHAW PATENT

with photographs by WILLIAM MUÑOZ

Houghton Mifflin Harcourt
Boston | New York

All images by William Muñoz with the exception of the
following: pp. 7, 9, 21 (both), 71 by Erick Greene;
pp. 15 (both), 24 by Kate Davis; p. 20 by Matthew Meier;
pp. 25, 72–73 by Dorothy Patent; p. 26 (top and middle) by
Word Museum of Mining; p. 26 (bottom) by
Demmons_013_Archives Library, University of Montana;
p. 29 (both) by EPA; p. 33 by Michael Kustudia and Gary
Matson; p. 46 (left and right) by Gene Miles; p. 60
(top right and bottom right) by Ashton Clinger.

www.hmhco.com

Design by Ellen Nygaard
The text of this book is set in Tiempos, Helvetica Neue,
and Tekton.

Library of Congress Cataloging-in-Publication Data

Patent, Dorothy Hinshaw, author.
  The call of the osprey / Dorothy Hinshaw Patent ; with
photographs by William Muñoz.
    pages cm. — (Scientists in the field)
  Audience: Ages 10–14.
  Audience: Grades 7 to 8.
  Includes bibliographical references.
  ISBN 978-0-544-23268-6
1. Osprey—Montana—Juvenile literature. 2. Osprey—
Effect of mining on—Juvenile literature. 3. Mercury—Bio-
accumulation—United States—Juvenile literature.
4. Pollution—Environmental aspects—Juvenile literature.
5. Wildlife conservation—United States—Juvenile literature. 6. Scientists—Juvenile literature. I. Muñoz, William,
illustrator. II. Title. III. Series: Scientists in the field.
  QL696.F36P379 2015
  598.9'3—dc23
  2014016090

Manufactured in Malaysia
TWP 10 9 8 7 6 5 4 3 2 1
4500509478

CONTENTS

Prologue   7

CHAPTER ONE
THE GREAT FISHER   10

CHAPTER TWO
DANGERS IN THE ENVIRONMENT   22

CHAPTER THREE
YOU ARE WHAT YOU EAT   32

CHAPTER FOUR
SPYING ON THE OSPREYS   42

CHAPTER FIVE
AFTER THE OSPREYS HAVE GONE—
ANALYZING THE DATA   52

CHAPTER SIX
LEARNING WHERE THE OSPREYS GO   62

Postscript   70

Author's Note   72

To Learn More   74

Sources and Acknowledgments   78

Glossary   79

The roofing truck lifts Erick Greene and Heiko Langner up to check on and clean the video camera that will bring the lives of the ospreys into homes around the world.

Prologue

On a cold day in March of 2013, Bill Muñoz, a photographer, and I drive up to the Riverside Health Care Center, a nursing home and skilled nursing facility just east of Missoula, Montana. We're meeting Erick Greene and Heiko Langner, scientists from the University of Montana, and Matt Young, their assistant. We shiver as we face into the bitter wind and head for the tall metal pole at the edge of the parking lot. On top of the pole is a flat platform with the remnants of an osprey nest and an extension on one side that holds a video camera. The three men are there to reactivate the camera after the long winter in anticipation of the April arrival of Iris and Stanley, a pair of ospreys that nested there the previous season. At least they hope Iris and Stanley will show up, since they proved to be outstanding parents. Ospreys mate for life, but a lot can happen in the seven to eight months that the birds spend thousands of miles south, in Mexico or beyond. Stanley and Iris had attracted many fans around the world to their webcam, and those people were eagerly awaiting the stories that would come with the new breeding season.

7

This webcam and another one south of Missoula are a boon to the long-term Montana Osprey Project, research the scientists have been carrying out since 2006, along with Rob Domenech, a fellow scientist. This study focuses on what has been the largest Superfund site in the country, an area that includes a 120-mile stretch of the Clark Fork River running from the mining town of Butte, Montana, to the former Milltown Dam a few miles east of Missoula. The Superfund project aims to remove the millions of tons of mining waste contaminated with heavy metals and to restore the natural environment. The scientists are using ospreys, birds that consume fish they catch in waterways near their nests, to evaluate the types and amounts of contaminants in the river. By analyzing samples of blood and feathers from osprey chicks being raised in twenty nests along the Clark Fork and its tributaries, the researchers can tell which toxic metals still linger in the system and where they are concentrated. They also use the project as an opportunity to educate the public about the natural world through the two webcams and visits by students and summer campers to the nests.

Erick and Heiko climb aboard the platform that the big red and white roofing truck will lift up to the camera. After donning safety harnesses and helmets, the two men are hoisted up as Roy Van Ostrand, the truck driver, expertly guides the platform over to the nest pole. Working on the camera in the cold Montana weather is not a pleasant chore, as the men need to use their bare hands to adjust the camera. Bill and I shiver as we crane our necks to watch the scientists patiently labor to make sure the camera is working well.

Once they return to the ground, it's our turn for a lift. I'm afraid of heights and had felt a bit leery as I watched the platform sway in the wind, but Heiko waves at me to come over. I hesitate, but he calls out with a smile, "Come aboard, it's part of the project. Besides, it's fun." "Okay, I'm coming," I answer, and join the men.

Bill and I don the harnesses and hard hats and up we go, soaring beside the swiftly churning Clark Fork River below, where the ospreys catch fish. We hunker down inside our coats, trying to avoid the cold wind as it gently rocks the platform. Despite the swaying, I'm not at all afraid; Heiko was right—this is fun. Roy expertly swings the platform up close to the empty nest, and I peer down to examine what's left from last year. I'm surprised to see little more than an almost flat surface of compacted material with some sticks encircling the diameter. I can see that the birds will have a lot of work to do to build a proper nest here once again, and I look forward to watching them, thanks to the webcam. Roy swings the platform down again and I exit quickly, rubbing my icy hands together in a vain attempt to warm them.

I'm glad to get back to my car, where I turn on the heat right away. Once home, I check my e-mail, and there's already a message from Erick, with attached photos of me and Bill on the platform titled "High on Life." I know I'm going to enjoy being part of this project.

It's clear that the birds will have a lot of work to do fixing up their nest this year.

Dorothy and Bill go up to take a look at the Hellgate osprey nest.

9

CHAPTER ONE

THE GREAT FISHER

I t's a warm, sunny afternoon in early May at the Riverside Health Care Center, where Erick Greene greets a group of students from Hellgate High School in Missoula. They have come to learn about ospreys, birds whose giant nests decorate the tops of dead trees and nesting platforms along the shores of rivers, lakes, and seas across the country and around the world, including in Europe, northern Asia, and Australia.

These young ospreys are growing up amid the mountains of Montana.

11

Erick Greene tells the high school students about ospreys.

Spreading the Word

The scientists work hard to spread the word about ospreys and the dangers of pollution in several ways. The visiting students are part of the flagship program of Missoula's Watershed Education Network (www.montanawatershed.org), a nonprofit offering young people information about the ecology of waterways in western Montana. The scientists are also part of the Bird's-Eye View Education Program, which carries out summer programs for children and adults that teach them about the effects of mining activities, the life along the river, river restoration, and similar topics. Since these efforts have begun, thousands of young people and adults have learned about the environment along the river where they live.

As the students crowd around, Erick holds up a stuffed osprey with outstretched wings, its sharp talons spread as if about to snag a trout.

"There's no other bird quite like the osprey," Erick explains. "These birds are related to hawks and eagles, but they've evolved as specialists to capture fish. See this toe? It's flexible and can be turned backward to help grab the sides of a fish. The toes also have these small rough spines that help grip slippery fish securely. And all the toes are the same length and have especially strong and sharp talons. An eagle's foot is very different from this one—its toes vary in length, and only one toe faces back."

Erick picks up an osprey skull and points out the beak. "See how sharp and curved it is? This

A student examines the osprey's skull closely.

helps the bird tear away the meat of the fish into small pieces to eat or to feed to its chicks. After the chicks hatch, you'll be able to see this for yourself on the webcam."

Erick shows with his hand how the osprey's powerful toes can reach out toward prey.

Erick shows a leg bone of an osprey and explains that these birds have especially long legs for reaching into the water to grab their prey.

A successful hunter, a fish grasped in his talons, heads back to the nest.

He picks up a wing bone next and lays it down along the stuffed bird's wing. "Like all flying birds, ospreys have very lightweight bones. The wings look big, but that's because of the feathers that are arranged to help the bird soar and dive. The wing is mostly feathers.

"See how short the body feathers are? You can't really tell with this dead bird, but the feathers are also especially oily so they repel water and keep the bird from getting waterlogged when it plunges after its prey.

"Here's how the bird hunts," Erick explains, using his arms to demonstrate. "It soars over the water looking for fish. When it spots its prey, the bird hovers in place as it zeroes in, then tucks its wings into tight V's above its back as it dives steeply downward. Its talons stretch out and its head reaches out in front. Then it tips its tail this way and that to make small adjustments in the dive. It hits the water with a big splash and disappears in the spray for a few moments as it grabs the fish. Then off it goes, its wings sweeping downward and forward, pulling it out of the water, dinner firmly grasped in its talons. Now, that's some bird!"

Iris's nest used to be here, where she and her family constantly risked electrocution. Notice the plastic triangles that now discourage birds from nesting here. There's also a fake owl intended to scare away birds, but the ospreys aren't fooled—Stanley sometimes perches on the owl's head!

Erick leads the students up a slope that overlooks the Clark Fork River. "See that power pole over there by the river?" he asks, pointing toward the pole. "That's where the ospreys used to nest. But power poles are dangerous—if the bird's wings touch two wires at once, it gets electrocuted. The nest was moved and the birds are now much safer."

The new platform for the Hellgate osprey nest went up during a winter storm.

A plaque honoring Mary Torgrimson Olson gets mounted on the pole.

Moving the Nest

A woman named Mary Torgrimson Olson used to live at the Riverside Health Care Center. She loved watching the ospreys on their nest on the power pole, but she worried about them. When she died, her daughter, Karen Wagner, decided to do something about the situation. She talked to Kate Davis, director of Raptors of the Rockies (www.raptorsoftherockies. org), who had been giving presentations about raptors to Riverside residents. Kate knew that the power company, Northwestern Energy, didn't like birds nesting on their poles, so she asked for their help. Raptors of the Rockies bought the first webcam, since replaced. That camera was set up with the cooperation of the Riverside Health Care Center and help from Northwestern Energy. Karen helped out with a contribution to Raptors of the Rockies. The nest was moved to its present location, and ever since, people, including center residents and the scientists, could watch the birds up close and personal.

The students walk over to the parking lot, and Erick shows them the sturdy nest pole. "Now the birds can nest here safely, and they're still close to the river," he says.

In the Health Care Center lobby, Erick shows the group the webcam image of an osprey sitting on the nest. "We call her Iris," he says. "She arrived back from her wintering spot a few days ago, and now she's waiting for her mate. We call him Stanley. Last year, they raised three healthy chicks in this nest, and we hope they can do the same this year."

Erick shows the students how he can move the camera around and focus in to see details of the nest and the bird. "This camera lets people anywhere in the world with Internet access follow the story of this osprey family whenever they want. You can watch them too, from your home or at school."

After the students leave, Erick packs up his gear and heads to work at the university, hoping that some of the students were inspired by this field trip to follow the story of Iris and Stanley and to care about wild animals like ospreys.

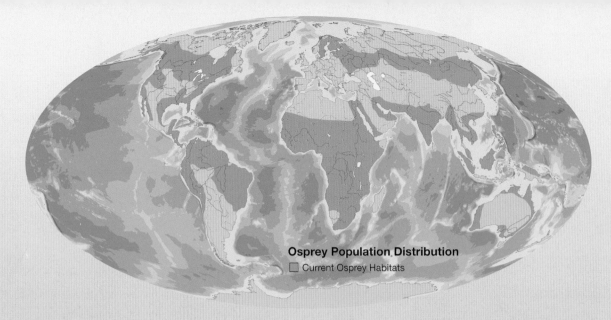

Osprey Population Distribution
☐ Current Osprey Habitats

Erick shows the students the image from the nest on the television in the Health Care Center lobby.

Iris got her name because her left eye has a unique pattern, with a few dark spots within the yellow iris.

Osprey Stats

Scientific name:

Pandion haliaetus

Color: Adults are very dark blackish brown on their back and wings, with a white breast, variable white with dark markings on the neck and upper breast, and a dark stripe through the eye. The young have white edging on the back and wing feathers and, when just out of the nest, a buffy color on their breasts and back of neck that fades with time. The tail is banded with black and white. When ospreys fly, each wing is often arched and partially bent into a V shape.

Size:
Males: 2½ pounds (1.1 kg) to 3½ pounds (1.6 kg)
Females: Up to 4½ pounds (almost 2 kg)

Wingspan: Up to 6 feet (1.8 m)

Life span: Up to 20 years

Family size: Female lays 1 to 4 eggs

Incubation period: 5 to 6 weeks

Eggs: Creamy white to tan with brown or reddish-brown blotches

Eye color:
Adults: Yellow
Young birds: Amber

HAVING A FAMILY

Ospreys usually return to the same area every year and meet up with the same mate, generally raising the family in the same nest. An unmated male performs a dramatic "sky dance" display to attract a female. He flies overhead with impressive dips and dives, rhythmically calling "eeeet-eeeet-eeeet." Most often, he carries a fresh fish or a choice piece of nesting material, such as a large stick, in his talons as he displays. The female waits at the nest site, checking him out. If she chooses him, she begs him to feed her as if she were a young chick. It's important for her to pick a mate who can fish well, for she and the chicks will depend on him for food until the young birds learn to fly and fish for themselves.

As soon as they arrive back at their breeding areas, the male and female build or repair their nest together, carrying sturdy sticks to form the main structure and softer material for the center, such as grass or tree bark. They are particular about the nest, using their beaks to reposition branches and to shred pieces of bark into soft, fine fibers. During the time they are fixing up the nest, the pair mates several times. The male spends more time bringing nesting material while the female arranges the nest.

The parents take turns incubating their eggs, but the female spends more time on the nest than the male. They each have a bare patch of skin on the breast that they snuggle up against the eggs, keeping them warm. (Feathers act as insulation, holding in body heat, so they could interfere with incubating the eggs.)

Both the male and the female help build the nest.

Even during a spring blizzard, Iris sticks to the important job of incubating her eggs.

The female feeds the chicks while the male keeps an eye out for trouble.

Osprey eggs are speckled with reddish-brown spots that help obscure their shape, making them harder to see tham pure white eggs.

Each chick has a white egg tooth on the beak that helps it peck its way out of the shell.

The chicks are losing their down and growing new feathers.

When a chick is ready to hatch thirty-five to forty days later, it uses a pointed egg tooth at the tip of its upper beak to break through the shell. The chick is helpless and awkward at first, but gains strength fast. Its body is covered by soft light gray or tan down, and its eyes open within a few hours of hatching. From the beginning, the chick can take food from its mother's beak, opening wide for her to poke the tidbit in.

After the male brings a fish to the nest, the female grasps the meat, twisting her head back and forth to tear off each piece of flesh to feed to the chicks. By ten to twelve days of age they have grown a thicker coat of gray and white down feathers. Well-fed chicks grow fast. By the time they are a month old, they have already reached 70 to 80 percent of their adult weight. By then, their feathers have grown in and they look much like adults, except for the white edging on their dark feathers and the pale brown feathers around their necks. This feather pattern makes the chicks hard to see in the nest. Great horned owls and golden eagles are big enough to attack young ospreys, and if danger threatens, the young birds crouch down in the nest and remain completely still.

Soon the youngsters start exercising their wings, standing on the edge of the nest and flapping until they lift off a bit, then settle down again. They start feeding themselves from the fish their parents have brought to the nest, and spend more and more time working their wings. By seven to eight weeks of age, they are able to take short flights away from the nest but then return. Bit by bit, they are growing up.

Finally, once they can fly, the young birds need to learn how to fish. It's August or September by then, and the female parent usually takes off and heads south, leaving the male to help the chicks learn to fish. Catching fish isn't easy—it usually takes a couple weeks of practice before the chicks are successful often enough to feed themselves, and it may take years to get really good at it. At this time, the father may leave, but the young birds often stay around longer, then head south on their own. They somehow know to fly south, looking for a good place to spend the winter. Ospreys living in places like Florida, where winters are mild, don't migrate.

Can you find the chick hunkering down and staying still?

Time to test those wings!

Osprey Migration

Ospreys in warm climates such as parts of Australia and Florida stay put for the winter. But the vast majority of the world's ospreys leave their breeding grounds and head south. The strong osprey wings can carry them more than three thousand miles (5,000 kilometers) in search of a good place to spend the winter. Once they have arrived, by the end of November at the latest, the birds tend to stay in one area until it's time to return to the breeding grounds beginning in late February or early March.

Ospreys tend to cluster in particular areas during the winter. For example, birds breeding in Finland and Sweden often spend the winter along the African coast from Senegal to Cameroon. Most American ospreys overwinter in Central America and northern South America. Once an osprey has found a good place to spend the winter, it usually returns there every year.

As spring approaches, ospreys begin their journeys back north. Adults seem to be in a hurry to get started on their new families, taking half to a third as long getting back as they spent flying south. Young birds stay put in the wintering grounds until they are at least two years old. Some two-year-old ospreys also return to the north, but more slowly than breeding-age birds.

Even populations of ospreys that

Ospreys from Montana may fly

LIVING IN COLONIES

Like many other birds, ospreys often nest close together on islands. Erick Greene got hooked on ospreys as an undergraduate honors student at Dalhousie University in Nova Scotia. Stationing himself on a bluff overlooking an island in the Cow Bay estuary, he watched as the island nesting birds flew off to hunt for fish and kept track of the direction the birds chose to fly. He found that male birds watched one another as they returned to their nests carrying fish.

"It's amazing," Erick told me. "Ospreys have such great eyesight, they can tell what kind of fish another bird is carrying long before it gets close to its nest and way before I could recognize what kind of fish it was." And if that bird was carrying a fish that travels in schools, such as an alewife or smelt, the watching bird almost always took off in the direction the successful hunter came from, as there was likely to be more fish in the school. If the returning bird carried a flounder, on the other hand, the perched bird didn't necessarily fly in that direction.

"Flounder," Erick explained, "live as individuals—not in schools. They're flat and hidden by their color on the bottom of the estuary. They are scattered around randomly, so if an osprey catches a flounder in a certain place, that information would not help another hungry osprey catch a fish."

This osprey nest overlooks Cow Bay estuary.

Above: A male osprey at the Cow Bay site brings home a pollock for his mate.

21

CHAPTER TWO
DANGERS IN THE ENVIRONMENT

Ospreys have few predators. They are big and strong and have powerful talons and sharp beaks to defend themselves. But even ospreys sometimes must contend with other creatures.

Osprey eggs are a tempting treat for some predators. In North America, raccoons have been known to raid osprey nests. These smart and agile animals climb trees easily, but they have trouble reaching nests on tall metal poles. Large predatory birds, however, can prey on exposed osprey nests, and ravens will snatch unprotected eggs from a nest. Great horned owls can attack, and even great blue herons have been seen raiding a nest. Bald eagles may prey on an osprey nest and are suspected of killing adult ospreys that nest too close to the eagle's territory. In northern Europe, eagle owls may kill osprey chicks.

Iris and Stanley's nest is near busy parking lots and not far from a road and a railroad track, but they are used to the human activity. The University of Montana is constructing a new building on the land behind the nest. During the construction all care will be taken to not disturb the nest. A park is planned for the area around the nest.

DDT

DDT is short for dichlorodiphenyl trichloroethane, a colorless, tasteless, almost odorless gas. It was first created in a laboratory in 1874, but it wasn't until 1939 that the Swiss chemist Paul Hermann Müller discovered it could kill insects. DDT was invaluable in World War II as a weapon against mosquitoes carrying deadly diseases such as malaria and typhus. It soon became popular as an insecticide on farms, and Müller received the Nobel Prize in Physiology or Medicine in 1948.

In her 1962 book *Silent Spring*, the biologist Rachel Carson expressed serious concern about the widespread use of DDT and other poisonous chemicals. DDT contains chlorine atoms attached to chains of carbon atoms. Chlorine can kill insects, but it can also damage other living systems.

When DDT accumulates in birds, it causes their eggshells to be paper thin. When the parent sits on the eggs to keep them warm, the thin eggshells break. The populations of many birds, such as ospreys and bald eagles, crashed because of DDT. In 1972, after DDT's effects on the birds became known, its use in American agriculture was banned. Today, it is still utilized in some parts of the world to control disease-carrying insects.

MINING AND THE ENVIRONMENT

In the early days of the colonization of the American West by European Americans, much of the population arrived because of the enormous reserves of important metals such as gold, silver, and copper that existed deep inside the mountains. People didn't think very much about the effects of their activities on the natural world, such as the lives of fish and ospreys, or even people—there was too much money to be made, and America's resources seemed endless. But mining operations that bring minerals from deep in the earth up to the surface can pollute waterways. Besides the useful metals, the mined rocks often contain minerals that become toxic to plants and animals. For example, chemicals in the rocks called sulfides can react with oxygen in the air or water to create sulfuric acid. The acid then causes "acidic mine drainage," the seeping of polluted water from old mine shafts and from piles of waste rock. When these seeps flow into streams, they can kill fish and other water animals and plants. The acid also dissolves large amounts of toxic metals from rock. The heavy metals are deposited into the sediment at the bottom, where they are picked up by bottom-feeding organisms and, just like DDT, are then carried up the food chain to the top predators such as bald eagles and ospreys.

Starting in the late nineteenth century, mining was a big industry in western Montana. First came mining for gold and silver. Then, at the end of the century, when electric power became common, mines in Butte, Montana, produced abundant copper, which is an especially good

The mines took over the town of Butte, Montana, in more ways than one.

The smelter in Anaconda, where most of the copper ore was processed, featured a giant smokestack. It was thought that a tall stack would send the smoke safely away from the town. The smelter is now gone, but the stack remains as part of a state park. The 585-foot (178-meter) stack is the tallest freestanding brick structure in the world.

The flood of 1908 sent hundreds of tons of mine waste down the Clark Fork River and over the dam, surrounding the power plant with water. Tons of waste were trapped by the Milltown Dam, but the dam couldn't hold back all the water.

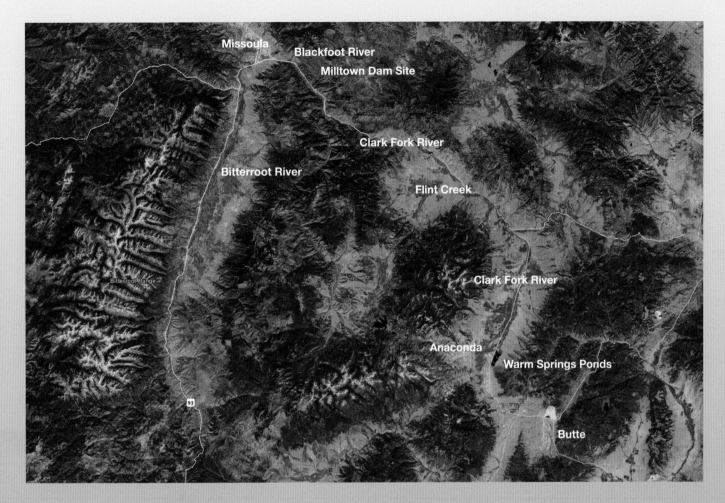

Missoula
Blackfoot River
Milltown Dam Site
Clark Fork River
Bitterroot River
Flint Creek
Bitterroot Range
Clark Fork River
93
Anaconda
Warm Springs Ponds
Butte

The Superfund site encompasses many areas, including land in and around Butte and Anaconda, the Warm Springs ponds, the creeks that feed into the headwaters of the Clark Fork River, and the entire length of the river from the headwaters at the ponds to the Milltown Dam. Many areas have already been cleaned up, but most of the rehabilitation of the river itself is still under way.

The osprey study includes not only nests along the Clark Fork River but also nests on the Blackfoot River and the Bitterroot River, which are outside the Superfund site.

conductor of electricity. Butte became one of the largest cities west of the Continental Divide, attracting miners from all over the world.

The mines and smelters, where the ore is processed, in Butte and nearby Anaconda dumped huge amounts of poisonous waste into the headwaters of the Clark Fork River. The waste contained not only copper but also other toxic elements, such as arsenic, cadmium, lead, and zinc, sometimes so much that the water turned orange. During a record flood in 1908, millions of tons of poisonous earth were trapped behind

the newly constructed Milltown Dam just east of Missoula. Even more mining waste became "slickens," or deposits of the poisonous mine tailings along the Clark Fork floodplain, where almost nothing can grow. As time went by the poisonous waters of the river killed fish and other living things, creating an almost lifeless river.

In the early 1980s the mining era came to an end, leaving behind huge environmental problems, and in 1983, efforts to clean up the area created the largest Superfund site in the country. (See sidebar on p. 28.) The site

covered an area the size of the state of Connecticut and included Butte, Anaconda, much of the surrounding landscape, and the Clark Fork River from its headwaters west of Butte all the way to Milltown Dam, 120 miles (193 kilometers) westward.

What Is a Superfund Site?

Unfortunately, many human activities, such as mining and manufacturing, can leave behind dangerous materials. The Superfund program (www.epa.gov/superfund) is run by the U.S. government to plan and help pay for cleanup of such hazardous waste sites. The program also has the power to make the companies responsible for the pollution, requiring then to clean it up or pay for government cleanups.

The Superfund program was established in 1980 after the discovery of dangerous pollution in two neighborhoods, Love Canal and Times Beach, in the 1970s. Love Canal was a community in upstate New York built on top of an industrial dump site. Homes there became uninhabitable because poisonous materials leached into the ground, and Times Beach in Missouri became contaminated by a chemical called dioxin. Only the federal government had the power to deal with such complicated problems—moving families to safe living quarters, forcing polluters to pay for cleanup, and coordinating the process. Since then, the Superfund program has dealt with thousands of polluted sites across the United States, some small and others enormous, such as the Upper Clark Fork River project.

The complex cleanup of the disastrous contamination of the Love Canal neighborhood led to the creation of the Superfund.

The Warm Springs Ponds

The Warm Springs ponds were created in 1911 to treat the toxic water flowing from mining activities by way of Silver Bow Creek, which helps form the headwaters of the Clark Fork River. Over the years, lime has been added to the ponds, raising the water's pH to make it less acidic. This helps remove the dissolved metals by precipitating them out of the water into solid matter that settles on the bottom. The result is the creation of millions of cubic yards of toxic bottom sludge loaded with contaminants such as arsenic, cadmium, copper, lead, and zinc, but the water itself is clean enough to allow trout to live there and migrating birds to stop over safely.

The ponds are an important element in the Superfund cleanup, which has been largely successful so far. They have become both a wildlife habitat and a place for people to enjoy nature. However, major issues remain. Who owns the ponds, and who will take ultimate responsibility for them? Currently, the Montana Fish, Wildlife and Parks agency manages the fish and wildlife aspects of the ponds by way of a lease agreement with ARCO, the company that now owns the mining lands.

The Warm Springs ponds were created to help treat toxic waste from Silver Bow Creek, but already the damage to the river was severe. Also, the water from two other contaminated creeks still flowed freely into the Clark Fork River.

REMOVING THE MILLTOWN DAM

The Milltown Dam, just eight miles (13 kilometers) upstream from Missoula, Montana, on the Clark Fork River, created a number of serious problems for the region. The dam was built in 1908 to supply power for sawmills in the town of Bonner. The sawmills made wooden timbers that were used in the Butte copper mines. For a hundred years, the dam held back tons of mining sediment, poisoning the river and creating other problems as well.

For one thing, the arsenic contaminated people's drinking water. The copper poisoned fish. The dam had collected so much mine waste that in wet years, ice jams and spring runoff carried the toxic minerals over the dam. The dam itself was poorly constructed, and some feared it could break open and create a nightmare—a poisonous flood. Because of the complexity of the project, wrangling over dam removal took twenty-two years. But finally, in August of 2005, officials from four different government agencies, the Confederated Salish and Kootenai Tribes, ARCO (the mining company), and Northwest Power (which owned and operated the dam) signed the agreement that has resulted in the removal of more than thirteen thousand tons of toxic waste behind the dam and removal of the dam itself, as well as the restoration of the area to allow the Clark Fork and adjoining Blackfoot River to flow freely once again.

The Milltown Dam and the deposits behind it were removed starting in 2009. Now work is under way to remove the remaining contaminated earth along the river floodplain. However, there is no quick fix to such a prolonged environmental problem, and cleanup and restoration projects will continue into the future for more than a decade. Scientists want to know what effects the remaining remnants of toxic metals could be having on the ecosystem. Because they live along lakes, ponds, and rivers in the area and specialize in eating fish, ospreys have become a natural subject for research into the presence of heavy metals and related elements in the ecosystem and their possible effects on living things.

The Milltown Dam held back the water from both the Clark Fork River, on the right, and the Blackfoot River, on the left.

Removing the dam and the contaminated earth from behind it took years. This photo of work in progress was taken in 2008.

Meet the Scientists

Heiko Langner

Heiko was born in 1964 in what was then Communist East Germany—East and West Germany were at one point separated by the Berlin Wall. He studied tropical agriculture and, in the process, learned how to drive heavy trucks, a skill that has come in handy in the osprey work. He also served more than two years in the military. After the Berlin Wall came down in 1989 and visa restrictions were loosened, Heiko and his wife, a biologist, moved to Montana, where he got a Ph.D. in environmental science at Montana State University. His work there on soil chemistry led to a postdoctoral fellowship studying arsenic in rivers, a perfect lead-in to the Montana Osprey Project. Heiko is the laboratory chemist of the group.

An avid bicyclist, Heiko is happiest outdoors, riding his bike, hiking with his family, or cross-country skiing in the mountains. It's a busy family, with both daughters seriously into gymnastics. In the summer, Heiko really enjoys the process of tagging and sampling the osprey chicks. The rest of the year, he spends most of his workdays indoors as director of the Environmental Biogeochemistry Lab at the University of Montana.

Heiko loves being outdoors, especially when riding his bike.

Erick Greene

Erick grew up in Canada and got hooked on ospreys as an undergraduate while conducting his senior project observing the behavior of ospreys that nest in colonies. He's the biologist of the crew. Erick and his family used to live on a farm, where he and his wife did their best to raise the food the family ate. The family moved to Missoula in 1990. Both his daughters have studied biology, and the older is now a fourth grade teacher. His younger daughter is a graduate student studying desert frogs and toads. Erick's love of flying his Cessna airplane gives him a chance to see the osprey nests from above and check on the whole ecosystem very quickly. He flew Bill Muñoz over Butte and along the Clark Fork River so Bill could take photos from the air.

Erick enjoys working in the garden. Here he holds freshly dug potatoes.

His position as a wildlife biology professor in the Division of Biological Sciences at the University of Montana gives him the opportunity to study a wide range of subjects. Erick is especially interested in animal communication and how animals relate to their environments, with subjects ranging from caterpillars and flies to spiders and chickadees.

Rob Domenech

Rob, a wildlife biologist, got hooked on nature as a child, when he was fascinated by insects and spiders. Later on he developed a passion for raptors—hunting birds such as eagles, hawks, and ospreys. In 2004, he founded the Raptor View Research Institute in Missoula. When he has the time, Rob enjoys whitewater kayaking.

Rob sprays water on an osprey chick to keep it cool.

Every year, Rob travels up to mountain passes and ridgelines where raptors fly through during migration. He and his fellow workers have been applying blue vinyl wing tags onto golden eagles in order to track their flight paths and learn how far they travel, how long they live, and how they die. Rob's group places GPS transmitters (like the GPS in your car or on a cell phone) on ospreys as part of the Montana Osprey Study Project, which enables the researchers to follow their migration paths. Rob also takes part in the osprey banding and sampling.

Matt Young

Matt is an assistant in Heiko's lab, but he doesn't spend all his time there. He's a vital part of the banding and sampling team, gently removing chicks from nests, weighing them carefully, recording information on the blood samples, and slipping a needle into a tiny wing vein to collect blood.

Matt's main job in the field is handling the blood samples and recording the data about the chicks. Here he shakes up a blood sample.

Wildlife Biology Students

Without students, this research effort wouldn't succeed. During the short period when the osprey chicks can be tagged and sampled, the work schedule is intense, and each nest visit requires several people to succeed—gear needs to be carried, notes need to be taken, and at least one additional research team member is always needed to help hold down the chick's wing while the blood sample is taken. Since the osprey project started, dozens of students have been able to help out as research assistants.

Two students who have worked on the project, Anicka Kratina-Hathaway and Amanda Ormesher Schrantz, pose with osprey chicks before they are put back into their nest.

In the past, the students have been unpaid volunteers, devoting many hours to helping the project.

Now, because of the generosity of the Miles family and friends (see "For Love of the Birds" in chapter 4), two students can be paid for their time. The two students at the time of this book's writing are Allison Mills, who has taken on the project website, and Harrison Cooper, a talented artist who has helped with Google Maps.

Both Allison and Harrison have been invaluable members of the fieldwork team.

Harrison Cooper (on the left) and Allison Mills (on the right), recipients of the Taylor-Miles Award, stand with Peggy Taylor-Miles's husband, Gene Miles, and his son Andrew (see sidebar p. 46).

CHAPTER THREE

YOU ARE WHAT YOU EAT

I f you want to learn about contamination of rivers, just ask ospreys. They can't tell you directly, but their blood and their feathers can reveal what they've been eating. Since breeding ospreys feed on fish caught near their nests, the birds can tell scientists a great deal about how polluted the river is. Contaminated fish means contaminated osprey.

The birds get used to leg bands. The blue ones can be read from a distance using binoculars, giving scientists information about the locations of the birds.

The Clark Fork carries more water by volume than any other river in Montana. After collecting from streams in western Montana and Idaho, it empties into Lake Pend Oreille in Idaho. Its waters eventually end up in the Columbia River, which empties into the Pacific Ocean.

Banding Birds

The United States and Canada have been cooperating on a joint bird banding project since 1923. The Bird Banding Laboratory at the USGS Patuxent Wildlife Research Center in Maryland issues permits for banding programs. A lightweight aluminum band with a unique number is fastened onto a captured bird's leg, and information about the bird, such as location, age, sex, and other data, is sent to the central database at Patuxent. Then, if the bird is captured again or found dead and the tag is reported, that new information is added to the file. Over time, important information about populations, lifespan, reproduction, and cause of death for millions of individual birds is collected and can be analyzed. The information is vital for conservation and management of bird species.

The Superfund status of the Clark Fork River got scientists thinking about how to evaluate the health of the river's ecosystem. Rob, Heiko, and Erick banded together in 2006 when they realized that ospreys could provide the information they needed. Since then, they have been monitoring hundreds of nests in western Montana. They focus on osprey nests along the Clark Fork River, taking samples of blood and feathers from the chicks every year to check for heavy metals, and banding them to keep track of them after they leave the nest. Each year, they monitor as many nests as they can manage during the short period available. In 2012, they banded fifty-five chicks in twenty-four nest visits and in 2013, sixty-one chicks in twenty-seven nest visits. In 2014 the crew visited nine nests and banded twenty chicks. It's *exhausting* but rewarding work. Their first scientific results were published in 2011, and the studies are continuing. The team members not only sample the birds; they also collect sediment samples from many sites along the Clark Fork River to test for contamination. Both kinds of samples are tested for arsenic, cadmium, copper, lead, and zinc from the copper mining in the Butte area. The researchers include mercury as well because it had been used in processing silver and gold ore, which are also mined in the area. The sediment samples can reveal how much toxic material still lingers in the river, while the osprey studies show what quantities get passed through the food chain.

FIELDWORK

In July, the osprey chicks are big enough that leg bands will fit them and their blood can be sampled, so it's time for the scientists to go up on the roofing truck platform and pluck the chicks from their nests. Bill and I join them for three days of this work, accompanying the truck in my car. It's not always easy to get to a nest, so sometimes we end up inching and lurching slowly across a bumpy pasture or navigating a narrow truck path to reach the nest. Then we have to figure out how to turn around to get out once the work is done. We do our best to be quiet so as not to disturb the birds more than necessary, but the truck is quite noisy. The adult birds fly off the nest but stay around, circling and often calling in distress at the disturbance.

Some of the osprey nests are located along ranch roads and thus are not difficult to access.

Heavy Metal Dangers

Many heavy metals and related elements can cause problems for living things. They are found in our food, our water, and the air we breathe. Our bodies need small quantities of them to function well, but large amounts can bring about a variety of health issues.

Arsenic is the most poisonous of all, which helps explain why arsenic leaching into water wells along the shore of the Clark Fork River near the dam helped trigger dam removal. Arsenic can come not only from mining waste but also from the treated wooden ties used to support railroad tracks, which often run right next to rivers. Cadmium can harm various organs, including the liver and kidneys, while copper is especially poisonous to plants and also can damage the liver. Lead can spread quickly throughout the environment and injure various tissues, including bones and the brain, while excess zinc interferes with decomposition in soil and thus threatens the health of an ecosystem. Selenium is needed by living things in small quantities. It is a necessary part of some enzymes in the body, but too much of it can cause reproductive problems or even death. It is especially harmful to aquatic life. Mercury is dangerous because it is easily absorbed by living things. It can damage the nervous system and interfere with reproduction by injuring sperm and causing pregnancy problems or birth defects.

While some pollutants break down over time, losing their potency, elemental metals do not. Elements are the most basic units of chemistry. Once they are in a system, they stay there.

Train tracks often run along the shores of rivers. Unfortunately, toxic substances used to preserve the wooden railroad ties can dissolve in rainwater, which carries the contamination into the river.

Going up!

Many of the osprey nests in western Montana contain baling twine.

Dangerous Twine

A major hazard for osprey chicks is baling twine, the material used to hold together the bales of hay that farmers and ranchers feed to their livestock. In the wintertime, the ranchers drive out onto the range in pickup trucks loaded with hay bales. They cut the twine and drop the hay for feed. Most ranchers are very careful about picking up the leftover baling twine, but sometimes pieces end up in the fields. Ospreys love to pick up the twine and use it to line their nests. Since this rope is made of a form of plastic, it doesn't break down, and birds like ospreys see it as perfect nesting material. Unfortunately, the chicks easily become tangled and can't escape. In some areas, as many as 15 percent of osprey chicks die because of this problem. Even some adult birds get tangled and die. The researchers have found some amount of twine in almost every nest they visited. One nest that had blown down contained more than a quarter of a mile of this dangerous material!

Heiko carefully takes a chick from the nest.

For each trip on the platform up to a nest, Heiko, Erick, or Rob brings along a cooler for the chick or chicks. I'm happy to join Heiko on the platform, snapping on the safety belt and donning a hard hat. Up we go, as Roy, the roofing truck driver, operates the gears to raise the platform. We sway upward, and I watch as more and more of the surrounding riverside landscape comes into view. Heiko spots baling twine woven into the nest and signals to Roy. Roy carefully maneuvers the platform, and Heiko reaches out and yanks at the twine, doing his best to pull it out. He has to be careful not to damage the nest, so he cuts off the twine after removing as much as he can.

Roy then raises the platform to the edge of the nest. I crane my neck and peek in to see two osprey chicks, crouching down and motionless. Heiko reaches in and gently removes the chicks one at a time, placing them in the cooler and covering them with a towel. He nods to Roy, who slowly lowers the platform.

Back on the ground, the scientists and their helpers work quickly so they stress the chicks and parents as little as possible. They've set up their gear in the shade and are ready to spray the chicks with water to help keep them cool if necessary. Harrison Cooper takes a chick gently in one hand, smoothing its wings down along its sides and holding the scaly white feet, with their shiny curved black talons, out in front. Heiko motions me to come close so I have a front-row seat. He slips an aluminum tag onto the bird's right leg and uses pliers to anchor it into place. He picks up a blue plastic tag with one letter and one numeral and slips it onto the left leg, anchoring it with glue using a Q-tip. The blue tag can be read at a distance so that someone who sees the bird can report the ID information. Then he passes the chick back to Harrison, who tucks it into an old sweater sleeve to keep it quiet and compact while it is weighed. Another assistant writes in a yellow notebook, recording the numbers on the tags and the bird's weight so there's a record for each chick.

The work requires a number of tools for taking and storing the chick's blood, clipping a feather sample, and banding the chicks.

Heiko glues the blue tag together so it will stay on the chick's leg.

The blood sample is taken from a vein in the chick's wing.

Heiko takes over again and lays the chick on its back, slowly spreading the left wing out to the side. Heiko carefully moistens the inner wing joint with an alcohol swab, then gently feels for the vein. As he slips a tiny needle in to take a very small blood sample, I watch to see if the chick flinches, but it doesn't react to the needle at all. The crew works quickly so that the process of tagging, weighing, and sampling both chicks takes only about fifteen minutes. Then it's back up to the nest to return them to their home and on to the next location to repeat the process. Meanwhile, once we've left, the female osprey quickly returns to the nest, as does the male if he's nearby.

THE WORK CONTINUES

After joining the crew of scientists for two days, I wake up with a headache, probably from not drinking enough water on these hot, dry summer days. I feel much better after coffee and breakfast, so I drive off to the town of Drummond, an hour away. Western Montana consists mostly of small towns, each about an hour from its nearest neighbor. I'm meeting up with the group at ten, but they've been busy since six a.m., visiting nests around the area.

After arriving in Drummond, I call Heiko on my cell phone and follow directions to the nest they've just finished sampling. In addition to the big roofing company truck, our caravan consists of four cars—the university crew, Bill Muñoz, me, and two students from McGill University in Montreal, James Junda and Marianna Dimauro. The narrow tracks we must navigate to get close to the nests don't allow much room for turning around, so getting set to move from one location to the next takes lots of maneuvering.

Heiko and Sherilee Lund, who owns a ranch with an osprey nest along with her husband, are getting ready to go up to check out the nest. The ranch is rich with bird life—not only do several pairs of osprey nest in the area, but great blue herons and bald eagles do as well. Sherilee enjoys watching the birds and keeps track of their activities every year. She has introduced the scientists to neighbors and has always cooperated with the research. Ranchers like Sherilee are vital to the osprey project, since most of the nests the scientists study are on private land.

Our route for the next nest involves taking the service road alongside the freeway, then ducking through a narrow underpass consisting of a huge metal tube. We turn onto yet another narrow grassy track, but this one is more like a real dirt road. There's even room to pull our cars over to the side to park. The rancher who owns the land, Sherilee Lund, joins us, as does a minibus with children from a Montana Natural History Society summer camp. We must wait in the hot sun for the truck, which, because of its height, has to take a longer route. When choosing which nests to monitor, the scientists have to think about whether or not this big, heavy truck can get to the nest site.

Roy drives the truck farther down the road to position it by the nest, and the children, who range in age from about four to ten, scramble from the bus. Heiko talks a bit about the nest and the birds and introduces me; then James Junda takes over. James opens up a special case that contains a miniature helicopter and its gear, all nestled into custom niches to protect them during transport. The helicopter is about a foot in diameter, black and square, with a rotor at each upper corner. James attaches the camera to the bottom of the copter with Velcro.

"This camera takes a photo of what's beneath it every second," James explains. He uses his handheld control to demonstrate, and the helicopter rises magically from the ground and heads above the truck. We all gasp as the copter zips skyward, and we crane our necks to watch it become a dot in the sky, turning this way and that, up and down, depending on how James guides it. James can tip it a bit, but it has stabilizers that keep it from moving much beyond horizontal.

I comment to James, a master's student at McGill, that it must be fun to run the helicopter.

"Actually," he responds, "I'm always pretty nervous. It costs about seven thousand dollars and I have to be careful it doesn't get damaged."

James and Marianna have already visited this nest and peeked in via the helicopter, so we know there's just one chick.

Up goes Heiko on the platform to fetch the youngster. When he comes down, the children ooh and aah when they see the chick up close. They crowd around the felt blanket where Harrison Cooper sits waiting. "You have to be really quiet," Heiko tells the children. "We don't want to upset the chick any more than necessary."

As he works, Heiko quietly explains what he's doing. Because this nest has only one chick, the procedures go quickly, and Heiko has time to hold this quite mellow chick gently in his hands while the children gather around for a group photo. Sherilee joins Heiko on the platform to return the chick to the nest.

Now it's time to say good bye to the campers and move on. The roofer truck has begun slowly rumbling back down the road toward the third Drummond nest. We turn our cars around and go back the way we came, taking a turnoff to the right past the town, then left onto a road along the old railroad bed, just wide enough for a barely visible car track through the knee-high weeds.

Sometimes railroad rights-of-way have been turned into narrow dirt roads, making it possible to get to an osprey nest. It can be hard turning around when it's time to leave.

James demonstrates the helicopter to the children from the Montana Natural History Society camp.

The helicopter camera snapped this photo of the bus and people on the ground watching the copter fly.

39

This osprey's-eye view of the landscape shows the lush riverside and the birds' fishing grounds.

Heiko returns the chicks to their nest.

The truck is ahead of us and starts the process of mashing down the weeds. I'm second in the line of four cars. The undercarriage of my car is getting its best cleaning ever as the weeds brush against it making weird noises; they are much taller than the level of the car body. We stop our cars in a line back from the truck. I notice, with sadness, that even way out here, the plants I recognize are all nonnative—knapweed, Russian thistle, and others that have come here from somewhere else and taken over, replacing the native species. But everything here is still green, while the vegetation on the hills is getting brown from lack of rain; the water table from the river must be quite high.

I go up on the platform with Heiko, and he takes the two chicks from the nest. Because of the small amount of shade, the crew needs to squeeze in halfway under the back of the truck. While they are processing the chicks, I chat with James about the helicopter.

"I'm working hard to perfect my skills at guiding this gadget," James says. "It's exciting to think how many uses it could have in field biology studies. When I finish graduate school, I want to start a company and connect with researchers to show them how I can help them find information they couldn't get any other way."

I go up again when Heiko returns the chicks to the nest. I enjoy the sweeping view of the river and surrounding countryside for one last time. The researchers are continuing to visit nests in the area around the town of Ovando, a half hour away, but I need to get home.

Once we manage to get our cars turned around, we pull over once more so the researchers can take a sample from the river.

We tramp through five-foot-tall brush and over a barbed wire fence to reach the river.

"See these bright speckles? They are iron pyrite, part of the waste from the mine," Matt explains as he shows me a plastic bag containing the blackish muck they so desire.

"We need the finest river deposit like this stuff for our analysis," he says. The scientists take samples from a total of about fifty spots along the rivers that are close to osprey nests. Three sites that they sample every month have been sampled for twenty years—Deer Lodge, Gold Creek, and Turah Bridge. They chose spots just above and just below tributaries so they can compare and pinpoint where the heavy metals come from.

As I drive home, tired from just my short time with the group, I think about how hard they work—day after day for several weeks, they are up at five a.m. and out the door, driving from site to site, sometimes many miles apart in this rural landscape. They must band and sample the chicks while they are big enough for the procedure but still too young to fly, and in this hot summer, they must finish their work by midafternoon. It requires careful focus so as to limit stress to the birds and to keep all the details in order. I admire them, but I'm glad I can return home early in the day and get some rest.

Heiko scoops a sediment sample from the bottom of the river.

41

CHAPTER FOUR
SPYING ON THE OSPREYS

In 2011, the scientists and the public got an opportunity to check on the birds at two of the nests once the webcams were installed. It didn't take long before people discovered this chance to watch osprey family life up close and personal and at the same time interact with the team of scientists and others to learn about how the birds live. The ospreys that raise their family at a nest by the Riverside Health Care Center east of Missoula, Montana, near the mouth of Hellgate Canyon, have been named Iris and Stanley, while Ozzie and Harriet, named after a couple in an old television comedy, nest on a pole at Dunrovin Ranch, south of Missoula. With a page on Facebook, a university website, and a website that connects people at the Dunrovin camera and ranch, these ospreys have become known around the world. In 2012, the webcams received about a half a million unique views. Now each year, people eagerly await the key events in the lives of the birds—the arrival of "their" ospreys each spring, the laying of the eggs and hatching of the chicks, and the great devotion and care the parents show as their chicks grow, become self-sufficient, and leave at the end of summer to begin their independent lives.

Iris, Stanley, and their chicks on the nest.

In late summer, osprey chicks begin to fly. You can see a blue leg band on this chick as it comes in for a landing. The other chick is standing on the nest behind its mother, Iris.

THE ADVENTURES OF IRIS AND STANLEY

In 2012, as Iris and Stanley worked hard to raise three healthy chicks, thousands of people around the world followed their lives by watching the webcam pointed at their nest. The perfect osprey mate, Stanley helped Iris incubate the eggs while the chicks developed inside. After they hatched, he brought Iris and the chicks fresh fish on a regular basis, and the youngsters thrived.

When Iris showed up again in early April of 2013, webcam viewers held their breath waiting for Stanley to arrive. No one knew where either bird had spent the winter, somewhere far to the south, or even whether Stanley had survived the winter so far away. A different male osprey appeared and displayed interest in Iris, even mating with her, but he wasn't Stanley, and he wasn't acting like a good mate. He rarely showed up, and Iris would sit on the nest, calling out and getting no response. Then another male arrived, but he also didn't behave like a loyal mate, and he wasn't Stanley either. Stanley had appeared rather late in 2012—early in May—so maybe it was still just too early. But meanwhile, Iris had laid two eggs and sat alone on the nest, faithfully incubating them.

Things changed suddenly the first weekend in May. Stanley finally had found his way home to Iris, but he had to battle one of the other males to claim his mate. Then he shocked some webcam viewers by tossing out one of Iris's eggs and burying the other one deep within the nest. Everyone thought he was such a good mate, and here he was, destroying Iris's eggs. Then the next day, she laid another egg, which Stanley also disposed of.

It may be late April, but this is Montana and it can snow! Iris sits alone on the nest, waiting for Stanley to show up.

The snow is gone, but this male bird is not Stanley.

Finally, in early May, Stanley shows up!

Iris spends most of her time incubating the eggs.

Stanley and Iris's eggs in the nest.

Iris takes a bite from a fish Stanley brought while she's incubating.

It took Erick Greene's scientific explanation to cool off the concerned viewers. Erick pointed out to viewers online that from Stanley's point of view, those were the eggs of a stranger, and it would do him no good to spend his summer raising another male's chicks. He needed to pass *his* genes on to the next generation, not those of another bird—a very common concern for much of the animal world. Stanley wasn't making a conscious decision, of course, but his behavior achieved that goal. And after getting rid of those eggs, he mated often with Iris and kept adding new strong sticks to the nest. Perhaps a male osprey needs to mate and to work on building a nest before his fatherly instincts kick in.

When Iris next laid eggs, Stanley accepted both of them. Then began the long incubation period. The chicks hatched on June 1 and 2 and were promptly named Taylor and Miles in honor of Peggy Taylor-Miles (see sidebar on p. 46),

who loved the Hellgate ospreys. Taylor and Miles thrived under the excellent parentage of Iris and Stanley and grew into beautiful, healthy birds. By August 7, both were flying around the nest area, practicing flight, strengthening their wings, and learning how to fish. Once her chicks were launched, Iris departed for her southern winter home. She left on September 10, while Stanley stayed around until Taylor and Miles were on their way, about September 22.

Iris gently feeds her hungry chicks.

Almost time to leave the nest.

45

For Love of the Birds

Peggy Taylor-Miles loved the natural world, raising her three children in Oregon near the base of Mount Hood. The family had all kinds of animal pets, but Peggy was especially fond of birds. Her husband, Mike Taylor, made birdhouses and bird feeders to bring birds close to the home. He died in 2003, and Peggy later married Gene Miles, giving their blended family a home base on the Washington coast.

In 2012, Peggy was diagnosed with ovarian cancer. The chemotherapy exhausted her, but she had discovered the University of Montana osprey webcams. Watching the birds in their moment-to-moment lives, wild and free, inspired Peggy. She helped start a Facebook page called Friends of the Osprey in support of the project, helping thousands of people around the world discover the webcams. Meanwhile, the chemotherapy initially slowed her cancer, but it returned in early 2013. After she passed away, Peggy's family decided that the best memorial wasn't big bunches of beautiful flowers at a funeral. Instead, they asked people to honor Peggy's love of life and the birds by sending contributions to the Montana Osprey Project. So many people responded that a fund has been established in her honor to help pay students working on the study. In 2013, the two chicks at the Hellgate nest were named Taylor and Miles in her honor.

Peggy's daughter Jenne and her family came to see the ospreys for themselves and visited several nest sites.

Gene Miles and his son Andrew hold the plaque honoring Peggy's love of the ospreys.

The male and the female osprey cooperate in building the nest.

Watching the Webcam

The osprey webcams can make every one of us an intimate observer of daily animal behavior. The birds have no idea they are being watched and go about their normal lives. Here are some of my observations while watching the osprey webcams in 2013. Because they started their family earlier, I spent most of my time watching Ozzie and Harriet and their chicks.

April 5, around noon: Both Ozzie and Harriet have returned from their winter home and are busily rebuilding their nest. Harriet picks up sticks and moves them around, fussing over them. She chirps a lot as Ozzie returns with a nice big stick and places it around the outer rim of the nest. Both birds do a lot of chirping. They seem to have an idea of how they want the nest to look, and move sticks around to fit.

In addition to sticks, ospreys bring grass to make a soft bed for the eggs and chicks.

Sometimes they just stand on the nest together and look around. They chatter back and forth, mate quickly, and Ozzie leaves. By now the nest has a nice rim of sturdy gray twigs and an inside of soft material.

At about one p.m. Ozzie returns with a fish, and Harriet chirps with a different call as she takes the fish from him, grabbing it and flying off with it. Ozzie pecks at the soft lining of the nest, then tries to rearrange a long, bent branch.

Ozzie and Harriet work together on the nest.

After Ozzie leaves the nest, smaller birds appear on the nest and steal the soft inner material. These birds actually make their nests in the lower portion of the osprey nest. Both English sparrows and starlings are nesting in this "apartment house."

April 9–22: Both birds arrange the outer rim, working together to shape the nest. Together they create a strong, sturdy structure that can withstand the wind. The inside of the nest is filled with soft, fluffy material. I watch Harriet pulling strands from a piece of tree bark to create some of the soft lining, and see Ozzie bring in a ball of soft dark gray material, possibly dog hair. As they build, they "talk" back and forth using a variety of notes.

I really enjoyed watching the birds because they cooperate so well to create this big, strong nest. I also loved seeing the small birds sneak up and steal nesting material while the ospreys were away. Watching how Ozzie and Harriet interact and sometimes just hang out together shows how compatible they are as partners.

Harriet takes a fish Ozzie has brought for her.

April 24, 5:30 p.m.: Ozzie arrives at the nest, and Harriet gradually gets up from a sitting position to reveal an egg. Ozzie carefully moves in to replace her and begins incubating. A few minutes later he stands up and I can see two eggs! He pokes at the nesting material around them. Harriet is still there, perched on the edge of the nest; then she flies away.

6:34 p.m.: Harriet returns to the nest and stands for a bit with Ozzie. He tries to mate with her, then flies away as she nestles down to incubate the eggs.

Harriet lays another egg on April 26. This routine of taking turns incubating and poking around, rearranging the nest, continues until all three eggs hatch between May 28 and June 1. SuzAnne and Sterling, the owners of Dunrovin Ranch, have a naming contest on Facebook for the chicks—the winners are,

Even during the night, Harriet pays attention to the eggs.

in hatching order, Percy, Hope, and Dilly. Last year, the birds' fans were very disappointed when none of Harriet's eggs hatched, so these names reflect the fans' views of the birds—Percy is short for *perseverance* and Dilly is short for *diligence*.

Harriet uses her sharp beak to tear bark into soft material to line the nest.

The first chick to hatch, named Percy, breaks out on May 26, a rainy day, and he's already hungry!

Harriet has her work cut out for her with three hungry mouths to feed.

Seeing eggs in the nest is exciting for all the people watching these birds on the webcam. Thousands of people from around the world come online to watch, and friendships form among the most devoted viewers.

May 8: At this point Stanley has just shown up at the Hellgate nest, but the birds at Dunrovin are busy keeping their eggs warm and protecting them. By the first of June, all three eggs at Dunrovin have hatched, and the parents move into high gear to feed their hungry brood.

June 6, 4:30 p.m.: The Dunrovin chicks are growing fast, at least two of the three. Harriet concentrates on grabbing bites of fish with her strong beak, then yanking back and forth to tear the meat from the carcass. She turns her head and places the food into the nearest gaping beak. The biggest chick, first-hatched Percy, is right up front, gorging himself, while Hope manages to get plenty of bites. I get very worried about the smallest chick. While the others are getting their gray feathers and being very alert, fuzzy, whitish Dilly just lies in the middle

Only three days later, Percy has really grown, but Dilly looks small and very thin.

of the nest, jerking weakly now and then. My husband, Greg, can't stand to watch and leaves the room. Finally, Dilly struggles over and begins to get some nourishment from Harriet's beak. Percy keeps nudging in and grabbing bites, but Dilly keeps at it.

I worry that Dilly won't make it. It's unusual for ospreys to be able to raise more than the one or two strongest chicks, and it looks like Dilly may be doomed.

July 1, 11:00 a.m.: It's a hot day, and Harriet has her wings spread widely, creating shade that protects the chicks from the sun. The researchers call her protective wings a mombrella. She sees Ozzie and calls out loudly while the youngsters poke their heads up. Ozzie lands with a small flopping fish. Harriet and the chicks crowd around while Ozzie stands to the side. The chicks don't eat very much this time—Ozzie must have brought in more fish earlier. Instead they seek the shade under Harriet's wings and tail while Ozzie and Harriet feed themselves.

Time to strengthen the wings and get ready to fly.

It's amazing—now the chicks are all about the same size. I call to Greg and let him know, and he's delighted. It looks like all three chicks will make it after all.

I don't manage to spend much time watching the webcams after this, but when I check in I'm amazed at how fast the chicks are growing. By mid-July, the chicks are standing on the edge of the nest, flapping their wings, gaining the strength they need to fly. Before the end of the month, they are on the wing. Now the nest usually looks empty, but once in a while one of the parents and a chick or two will show up for feeding or rest. Bit by bit, the time between visits by the birds gets longer and longer, until the nest stays empty, waiting for next year and another family to raise.

By late June, Dilly is just as big as his siblings.

CHAPTER FIVE

AFTER THE OSPREYS HAVE GONE— ANALYZING THE DATA

The ospreys fly south in late August or September, but the scientists' work has just begun. It's time to begin analyzing the blood and feathers collected from the chicks that year. All the analysis is done in Heiko's laboratory at the Environmental Biogeochemistry Laboratory at the University of Montana Geosciences Department. Heiko shows me the refrigerator where the blood is kept in small vials until it is analyzed.

"Preparing a sample for analysis takes quite a while," he tells me. "It's called 'digestion' and is a lot like the digestion of food inside our bodies. The blood cells and larger, solid particles in the samples have to be broken down into molecules that dissolve in water."

Matt Young adds concentrated acid to the blood samples. The acid will digest the blood, turning solid material such as blood cells into liquid. He has to do this under a laboratory fume hood because the acid releases toxic fumes. The hood pulls the fumes up and away and also prevents the room air from entering the space around the samples by blowing a curtain of air between the room and the inside of the hood. Not only does this prevent the toxic fumes from entering the room, it also keeps dust particles in the room from contaminating the blood samples.

Once the chicks have begun flying, the nest is often empty, but for a time the young birds return now and then. Once the family has flown southward for the winter, the nest remains unoccupied and becomes battered by rain, wind, and snow until the birds return the next spring to rebuild it.

53

He turns on the machine that shakes up the vials to mix up the materials that settle out from the sample during storage. It makes a loud "rat-a-tat-tat" sort of sound. "Once the sample has been mixed up again," Heiko explains, "we weigh out a one-gram sample. Then we add nitric acid and heat the sample. This destroys the blood cells and makes some of the material water soluble. After that, we cool the samples, add hydrogen peroxide, and heat them once again, which finishes the process. The last thing we do before analyzing the sample is to add deionized water to bring the sample up to a volume of fifty milliliters."

We walk across the hallway to an unlabeled closed door. "This is what we call a 'clean room,'" Heiko says. "The air inside is filtered to remove any dust and other airborne particles that might contain traces of metals. The air pressure in the room is also kept higher than outside so there won't be any flow of unfiltered air into the room when the doors are opened. Most of the equipment, like fume hoods and water faucets, is made of plastic, or is coated to minimize any exposed metal surfaces that could be the source for contamination of samples. All these precautions are necessary so that we can accurately measure even the lowest levels of contaminants in the collected samples."

Finally, Heiko shows me the equipment used to make the measurements—an inductively coupled plasma–mass spectrometer (ICP-MS)

In the clean room, Matt carefully measures out one-gram samples of blood for analysis.

for the arsenic, cadmium, copper, lead, and zinc concentrations, and a cold vapor atomic fluorescence spectrometer (CVAFS) for the mercury. The CVAFS shines light on the mercury atoms, which then emit light in all directions. The amount of light reveals the quantity of mercury present in the sample.

Heiko then shows me the automatic pump used to inject a sample into the ICP-MS and points to the little transparent chamber where the sample is turned into a sort of fog before being carried into the measuring chamber that contains the magnets.

"The machine heats up the sample and strips away electrons from the elements, creating ions that vary in mass, depending on the element. The concentration of each element present can then be determined because each mass reacts differently when it travels through a magnetic field," Heiko explains.

Heiko holds up a sample that is ready for analysis. About one gram of blood is now completely dissolved in fifty milliliters of acid. More than a hundred samples are waiting to be analyzed.

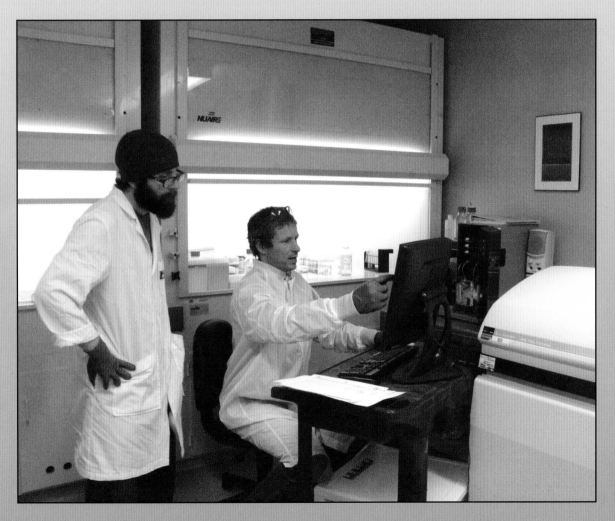

Heiko and Matt check the results of the CVAFS (with the green light against the wall) while the ICP-MS in the foreground waits to be used.

PUBLISHING THE RESULTS

In 2012, the first results from the study (compiled from 2006 to 2009) were published in a scientific journal. The researchers found that lead isn't passed up the food chain into the ospreys in significant amounts and neither is copper. Arsenic seems to be excreted from the birds' bodies quite quickly, and the birds also seem to be able to get rid of excess zinc. Thus, any residual amounts of major minerals from the Superfund site appear not to be a problem for the ospreys directly, although these contaminants cause fewer fish to survive and thus have an indirect effect on the birds because they find fewer fish than in a clean river. However, there was a surprise in the results: mercury, which is not connected with copper mining, showed up in potentially damaging concentrations in both the blood and the feathers of the chicks farther down the river. Where did it come from?

The answer lies in *another* kind of mining. The scientists chose to take their sediment samples from locations both above and below

Today, Flint Creek is surrounded mostly by farms and ranches.

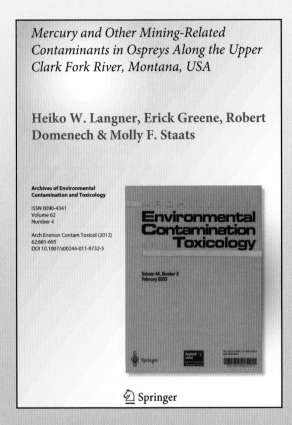

Mercury and Other Mining-Related Contaminants in Ospreys Along the Upper Clark Fork River, Montana, USA

Heiko W. Langner, Erick Greene, Robert Domenech & Molly F. Staats

Archives of Environmental
Contamination and Toxicology

ISSN 0090-4341
Volume 62
Number 4

Arch Environ Contam Toxicol (2012)
62:681-695
DOI 10.1007/s00244-011-9732-5

ARCHIVES OF

Environmental Contamination Toxicology

Volume 44, Number 2
February 2003

Available
online

Springer

The first article about the Montana Osprey Project study is in this journal.

where some tributaries enter the river. Because of this research method, they can pinpoint whether that tributary is a source of contamination. If the concentration above the mouth of the tributary is low but is high after the tributary joins the river, the source of contamination must be the tributary itself. It turns out that most of the troublesome mercury appears to come from a stream called Flint Creek, which enters the Clark Fork from the south side. A great deal of gold and silver mining occurred in Flint Creek from 1864 until

1945. Mercury levels in the Clark Fork River below the mouth of Flint Creek are five times higher than those above it. Unfortunately, Flint Creek is not part of the Superfund site, but the state of Montana is working on the problem as part of the Abandoned Mine Lands program.

METHYL MERCURY

The element mercury (Hg) in pure form is dangerous if it forms vapor in the air or if we breathe it in with dust particles, as when a fluorescent light bulb breaks. Otherwise, it's not especially hazardous. However, when mercury joins with what's called a "methyl group"—a carbon molecule attached to three hydrogen molecules—it becomes highly toxic. It affects the immune system, alters genetic and enzyme systems, and damages the nervous system, including our ability to think, our coordination, and our senses of touch, taste, and sight. Methyl mercury is particularly damaging to developing embryos, which are five to ten times more sensitive than adults. Methyl mercury is produced from other forms of mercury by bacteria that live in stagnant water and in the sediment of lakes, marshes, and other bodies of water.

The main risk of mercury contamination for people and wildlife is through eating fish that come from contaminated water. Whereas some dangerous contaminants, such as dioxins, become concentrated in fish skin and fat, methyl mercury goes into the meat of the fish, the part we eat. It's difficult to uncover effects of methyl mercury on wildlife, but so far several problems in the United

Methyl mercury forms in stagnant water such as this quiet spot in Metcalf National Wildlife Refuge.

States are documented, including fewer loon chicks in contaminated Wisconsin lakes. The adult ospreys in the Montana study spend many months a year away from Montana, so they could also be picking up mercury from fish at their winter homes. This makes it difficult to be sure how much methyl mercury the adults got from their breeding grounds versus their winter habitat. The osprey chicks, however, have only eaten fish that were caught near their nests. So by focusing on mercury levels in the chicks, the researchers can determine how much of a problem the contamination in Montana poses.

Fish from the River: To Eat or Not to Eat

Now that we know there's increased mercury in the Clark Fork River below Flint Creek, what does that mean for people who love to fish? If they are catching fish to eat, they need to be careful! Mercury is especially dangerous to women who are pregnant or might become pregnant, as mercury is very toxic to a developing fetus. The Montana Fish Consumption Guide says that above Flint Creek, men can safely eat as many whitefish of all sizes as they want, but women should limit how many they consume. For fish caught below Flint Creek, however, even men must limit what they eat, and women should eat little or no whitefish to be completely safe.

Many people enjoy fishing and eating the fresh catch. But in many places, fish can be contaminated by mercury and be unsafe to eat.

Below: You can see a coal train passing by across the road in this photo from 2012, when Stanley and Iris had three chicks.

The problem of mercury is further complicated by the fact that mercury can be carried from place to place in the air. For example, coal from Montana, which contains some mercury, is shipped to China, where it's burned to heat buildings. Burning releases the mercury, which then is carried on the wind back to the Unites States, including where it came from in Montana. There it settles on the plants, soil, and water and can enter the food chain even where there is no contamination from mining or other local sources.

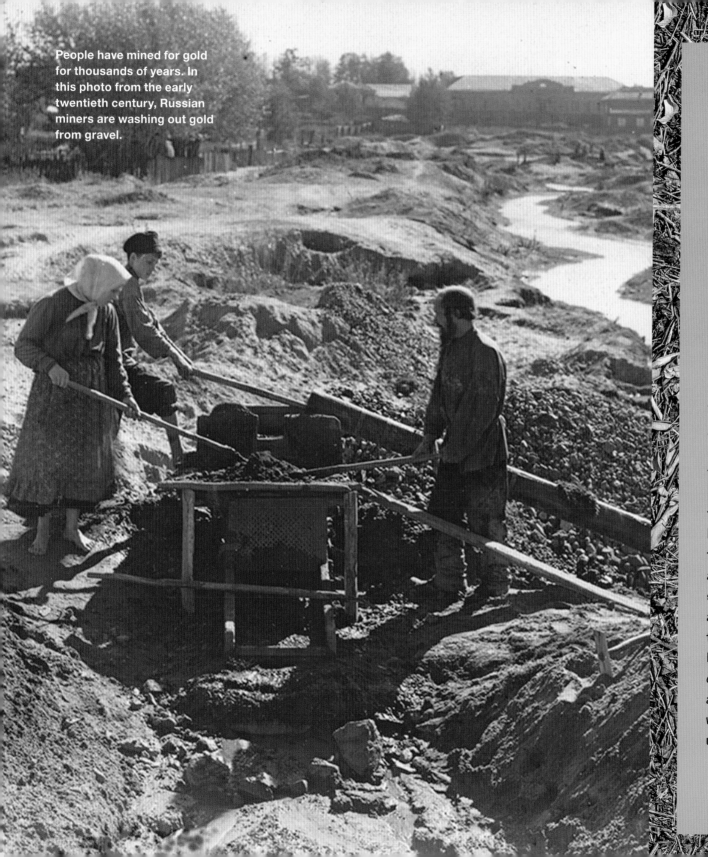

People have mined for gold for thousands of years. In this photo from the early twentieth century, Russian miners are washing out gold from gravel.

Mercury in Mining

Mercury has been used for hundreds of years of mining for gold and silver. Both of these precious metals can be extracted using mercury, which attracts the bits of gold or silver in mining waste or river gravel. This creates a pasty material called an amalgam. When the amalgam is heated, the mercury evaporates into the air, leaving the precious metal behind. The mercury vapor is dangerous as it can be breathed directly into the lungs. Not only that, but the process is very messy, and much of the mercury ends up in the water. Even though we know how dangerous mercury is to the nervous system, as much as a thousand tons each year are still used in Asia, Latin America, and Africa, as this process is the easiest way to extract gold. Mercury can travel for thousands of miles through the atmosphere and end up in rivers and oceans worldwide, where it can move up the food chain into fish.

A Scientist in the Making

Ashton Clinger became interested in the problem of environmental pollution by metals as a high school student in Cascade, Montana. She loved being on and in the water, and said about her study, "I would like to know what I'm jumping into." So she started by looking for arsenic in fish living in the Missouri River, and indeed, some fish were contaminated. Ashton decided to broaden her study to include other metals and another species besides fish. Ospreys were a perfect choice, both because she loved watching them fish and because of their fishy diet.

A teacher at Ashton's school, Ashley McGrath, had been an undergraduate student at the University of Montana and had studied under Erick Greene. When Erick and Heiko read the email from the teacher telling them about Ashton, they were delighted.

Ashton Clinger stands by the science fair display of her osprey study. She earned many merit awards at state and regional science fairs for her work, including the honor of participating in the International Science Fair in Phoenix, Arizona.

Ashton collects sediment samples from the Missouri River.

Ashton's work could provide valuable data about heavy metals and osprey from a completely different watershed across the Rocky Mountains from Missoula. Waters west of the Continental Divide ultimately flow into the Pacific Ocean, while those on the eastern side ultimately end up in the Atlantic Ocean. They are two separate systems.

No one had ever looked for contaminants along the thirty-five-mile (56-kilometer) stretch of the Missouri River that Ashton selected for her study. Mining isn't the only potential source for heavy metal pollution

The fish in this photo isn't glowing—its scales are just reflecting light from the camera's flash.

in that area. Interstate 15, with the accompanying potential pollution from vehicles, runs along the banks of the Missouri River. An abandoned railroad track also parallels the river, and arsenic is among the poisonous chemicals used to preserve wooden railroad ties.

Ashton joined in fish collection trips run by Montana Fish, Wildlife, and Parks researchers and was able to collect livers from three different species of fish in the river. In addition to sampling sixty-nine fish, Ashton got blood and feather samples from eleven osprey chicks being raised along that stretch of the Missouri River, and eight samples of the river sediment.

Ashton's samples of liver from the fish await analysis in the DMA.

Ashton uses an instrument called the direct mercury analyzer (DMA) instead of the CVAFS (used for liquid samples) to measure the mercury content of her solid fish and sediment samples. Here, Ashton programs the computer that controls the DMA.

Ashton's samples are still being analyzed, but no matter what the results, her work provides valuable baseline data—information that can be compared to further findings both in that area and across the Continental Divide. Heiko, Erick, and Rob hope that the future will bring more aspiring student scientists to expand and complement their studies.

Ashton is now a student at the University of Montana. "I want to become a fish and wildlife biologist," she says, "and I want to start by continuing this research while I'm a student. That way I can work and stay here in Montana."

CHAPTER SIX

LEARNING WHERE THE OSPREYS GO

At 8:30 a.m. on August 8, 2013, Bill Muñoz's phone rings. Rob Domenech of Raptor View Research Institute is ready to equip an osprey chick with a satellite transmitter. The chick is within a couple days of fledging, so the time has come. The birds need to be nearly full grown when given a transmitter so the straps holding it on don't get too tight as the chicks grow. Once the birds have left the nest it's too late, so there is only a short time period in which the satellite transmitters can be fitted.

It takes a good-size crew to handle the work of equipping the osprey chicks with satellite transmitters.

The MPG Ranch

The name MPG comes from the family initials of the owners. Although it's called a ranch, this property has no cattle. Instead, it is devoted to the protection and study of wildlife; the more than twenty employees include university-trained ecologists who work to rid the property of invasive weeds and reestablish native plants as well as study soil fungi and stabilize the soil. These efforts improve the land for the benefit of wildlife. The ranch also encourages other scientific research, such as the osprey study. Thirty onsite cameras sensitive to motion capture images such as a mountain lion (like the one shown below) carrying a deer it successfully hunted, nesting geese chasing off a coyote, wolverine, wolves, and rare spotted skunks, not seen in the valley for twenty years. The cameras send their images wirelessly to the ranch website, mpgranch.com.

Bill hops into his car, joins up with Rob and his helpers, and drives to the MPG Ranch, where the ospreys nest. While they wait for a couple of extra hands from the ranch to arrive, Rob explains to Bill, "When the birds are so near fledging, extra people are needed on the ground with nets just in case a bird jumps from the nest. These older chicks can move quickly. They are able to become airborne for a short distance but still can't quite fly, so this operation can be tricky."

Once the truck is in place, an assistant carrying a large net is hoisted up to the nest. He quickly captures the chick, bringing the net close to his body so the chick can't escape as the bucket is lowered to the ground. Rob and another biologist carefully remove the youngster from the nest and carry it over to a shaded area where they draw blood and weigh the bird. They mist it with water to keep it cool, just as with the younger chicks, except they place a hood over this older chick's head to calm it down.

Finally, the chick is outfitted with a satellite transmitter with a solar-powered battery. The transmitter will send a signal to the satellite far overhead every hour. The satellite then sends this information to the researchers' computers. This allows the scientists to track the young bird as it migrates and into the future.

One of the motion-sensitive cameras at MPG Ranch caught this image of a mountain lion on the move.

Time to net one of the chicks.

The female osprey gets upset by the human interference. The parent birds usually don't behave aggressively, so this is an exception.

The chick is hooded to help keep it calm and is sprayed with water to keep it cool.

"We have to be very careful putting on the transmitter," Rob tells Bill. "The harness can't be too tight, and it also has to be balanced so it doesn't affect the bird's flight."

Once the harness is in place, the chick is put back on the nest, where it can enjoy the fresh trout Rob placed there for it. As soon as the platform is lowered, everyone moves quickly away from the nest site but stays nearby, waiting until the female osprey returns to the nest.

Just as the researchers are driving out, they notice a group of mules acting interested in something caught up in a wire fence. It turns out to be a dead chick that Rob had outfitted with a transmitter the previous week.

Rob is troubled. Later on, he learns that the bird had sustained some kind of trauma, so the transmitter had nothing to do with its death. The researchers do their best not to cause any problems for the birds, but disturbing the nest and handling the chicks always carries some risk. Working with the older chicks is more stressful for both the scientists and the birds because they are larger and have passed the stage of life in which they just hunker down and stay still when disturbed. But the risk is worth it, for the transmitters can provide vital data about the birds' flight path and where they spend the winter. The only way we can help the ospreys survive as the world around them changes is by learning as much as we can about their lives.

Rob holds the bird, showing how the antenna that sends the signal to the satellite stretches out behind.

The transmitter rides on the back of the bird.

Rob examines the dead chick to see if he can figure out why it died.

You can see the antenna of the transmitter on this bird. She's the mother of the chick that got a transmitter in the fall of 2013.

The satellite transmitter worn by Rapunzel allows researchers to map her wanderings around the Pacific Northwest. Later on, she settled down in an area in northern Montana.

And so, in 2012, biologists from Raptor View Research Institute and the MPG Ranch began a project to uncover where western Montana's ospreys spend winter. At the time of writing, the five birds from two nests at the MPG Ranch wearing radio transmitters have overwintered in Mexico on the shores of the Gulf of Mexico, on the Mexican Pacific coast, and in Texas. One female flew all the way to the Nicaragua–Costa Rica border, where she spent the winter on a small Pacific Ocean bay.

The travels of one bird named Rapunzel illustrate the kinds of surprises that scientific research can uncover. Born in 2012, Rapunzel spent her first winter and the following year along the Gulf coast near Freeport, Texas. On May 11, 2014, she left her wintering grounds on the Gulf Coast, and headed north, passing within a few miles of her natal grounds just nine days later. But instead of stopping in Montana, she flew right over the nest where she was born and continued northward, all the way into Alberta, Canada, close to the United States border. Since then, she stayed on the move, logging thousands of miles in big loops—down through Montana, across Idaho, Washington, and Oregon, then back into Idaho, westward across Oregon and Washington, then northward into British Columbia and Alberta, back to Montana, then once again to Alberta. Then in August, Rapunzel settled down on a small creek on the Blackfeet Reservation in Montana. She spent most of her time fishing, probably storing up energy before her long southward migration. Before Rapunzel got her "backpack," scientists had no idea that an osprey would travel such distances looking for a place to settle down.

INTO THE FUTURE

Rob explains why this work is so important. "Our long-terms goals are to learn as much as we can about how and where these ospreys migrate and to compare the data with information from other parts of the country. Questions need to be answered: Do family groups and other birds from the same area use the same migration routes and wintering grounds? What are the similarities and differences in the chosen winter habitats of ospreys living in different parts of the country? And importantly, what human activities pose threats to ospreys? We can't help protect the birds if we don't have this kind of information."

One very important aspect of the study is to learn if there's a relationship between the mercury levels in the birds and their success in migrating, establishing a family, and raising chicks. We know that too much mercury can affect the nervous system—can we observe effects in birds that indicate high mercury levels? That information could take a long time to acquire, as only about 30 percent of osprey chicks survive their first year of life. Moreover, only a few birds have transmitters because of the expense. Still, if we discover that these birds have problems in completing their migrations, hunting for food, or raising families, that information could help us understand how pollution can upset natural systems.

Rapunzel (right) and her brother, Scooter (left), after being equipped with satellite transmitters and leg bands. Now their travels are being recorded so the scientists know where they travel after leaving the nest.

Postscript

In the summer of 2013, Erick wanted to get the word out more widely about the Montana Osprey Project. He submitted five short scientific papers to a conference of the Society for Conservation Biology that was going to be held in Bozeman, Montana. The conference would give students working on the project a chance to present the ongoing work and to meet scientists from around the country.

The results delighted Erick. Organizers for the conference were so excited that they set up a special session titled "Osprey Conservation" to highlight the osprey research. The students presented talks on the problem of baling twine, the use of satellite tracking to study migration, the heavy metal findings, the possibility that mercury could increase egg mortality, and the use of modern tools such as the webcams and Facebook to educate people about important environmental issues.

When the Montana Osprey Project began in 2006, very little was known about the ospreys living in western Montana. Now, thanks to these students and others, citizen volunteers, and the scientists working on the project, we know a great deal about these birds and their environment, and people around the world are familiar both with these particular ospreys and with the broader ecological issues involved in the osprey studies.

The research on the ospreys will continue. As data is analyzed over time, we will get a clearer picture of what's going on—how the excess mercury affects the chicks as they get older, how quickly the ecology of the Clark Fork River recovers, where the ospreys go to spend the winter, and what their survival rates are. Even as we learn more, there will probably be surprises in store for the researchers. But whatever facts these studies uncover, ospreys all over the world will continue to find their mates, build their nests, hunt for fish, and cry out over the waters of our lakes, rivers, and seashores with their unique rhythmic calls—*"eeeet-eeeet-eeeet."*

eggs is low in areas of high mercury.
, Harrison Cooper, Rob Domenech, and David Bird.

The students and scientists who attended the Bozeman conference hold up the baling twine removed from just one osprey nest. Baling twine was one of the topics covered in their talks. From left to right: Allison Mills, Erick Greene, Jay Egenhoff, Harrison Cooper, Adam Shreading, Heiko Langner, and Rob Domenech.

Other students involved in the research are Amanda Ormesher Schrantz, Matt Parker, Anicka Kratina-Hathaway, James Junda, Molly Staats, and Charles Eldermire.

73

TO LEARN MORE

BOOKS FOR YOUNG READERS

Patent, Dorothy Hinshaw, and William Muñoz (photographer). *Ospreys*. New York: Clarion Books, 1993.

Wechsler, Doug. *Ospreys (Really Wild Life of Birds of Prey)*. New York: Powerkids Press, 2001.

BOOKS FOR ADULTS

Carpenteri, Stephen D. *The Fish Hawk: Osprey*. Northword Wildlife Series. Chanhassen, MN: Northword Press, 1997.

Davis, Kate, Rob Palmer, and Nick Dunlop. *Raptors of the West: Captured in Photographs*. Missoula, MT: Mountain Press, 2011.

Dennis, Roy. *A Life of Ospreys*. Dunbeathm, Scotland: Whittles Publishing, 2008.

Gessner, David. *Return of the Osprey: A Season of Flight and Wonder*. New York: Ballantine Books, 2002.

Poole, Alan F. *Ospreys: A Natural and Unnatural History*. Cambridge: Cambridge University Press, 1989. NOTE: This was my resource for basic osprey facts.

INTERNET RESOURCES

There are many websites dealing with topics raised in this book. Here's a sampling of what's available.

MONTANA OSPREY PROJECT

- Website: www.cas.umt.edu/geosciences/osprey
- Facebook page: on.fb.me/1faVhQk
- Link to map showing travels of ospreys fitted with GPS transmitters: ranchmpg.apspot.com/ospreylocator.html
- Raptor View Research Institute: www.raptorview.org
- Raptor Facebook page: www.facebook.com/raptorviewresearchinstituteEducational project at Dunrovin Ranch: www.schooldaysatdunrovin.com

RELIABLE INFORMATION ON BIRDS

- The Cornell Lab of Ornithology has all sorts of great information about birds: www.allaboutbirds.org
- The National Audubon Society site also has plenty of information: www.audubon.org
- The Cornell Lab and National Audubon Society cooperate every winter in the Great Backyard Bird Count. Anyone can help out: gbbc.birdcount.org

HISTORY OF MINING IN THE WEST

- General history of mining in the West: www.westernmininghistory.com
- Specific information on Butte mining: www.westernmininghistory.com/towns/montana/butte
- History of mining in Montana: www.montanamining.org/water.htm
- Berkeley Pit: www.pitwatch.org

CLARK FORK RIVER CLEANUP

- This website for the Clark Fork River Technical Assistance Committee offers detailed information and photos of the various stages in the Superfund project: www.cfrtac.org
- The Clark Fork Coalition site describes the Milltown Dam removal: www.clarkfork.org/water-watch/milltown-dam-removal-and-cleanup-project.html

Laysan albatross in Hawaii: bit.ly/1ixX5Y5.

Black stork cam in Hungary: www.unavitaverde.net/webcam-black-stork.

BIRD WEBCAMS

• The best source for webcams on birds is the Cornell Lab of Ornithology site. The link to the Hellgate Canyon webcam is cams.allaboutbirds.org/channel/27/Hellgate_Ospreys. This lab helps sponsor the osprey cams of the University of Montana and a number of others. Some, like the red-tailed hawk and great blue heron webcams, follow nesting birds during the spring and summer. Others are trained on bird feeders during the winter.

• The star of the lab's newest webcam (as of press time) is the Laysan albatross: bit.ly/1ixX5Y5. This great webcam comes from the Hawaiian island of Kaua'i, where these birds raise their families from February to July. Each pair raises one chick. One parent stays with the chick while the other flies as far away as Alaska or Japan to bring back digested squid. It may be gone for two and a half days while its mate cares for the chick. Dawn in Hawaii is around noon Eastern time, which is nine a.m. Pacific time.

OTHER WEBCAMS

• White storks in Hungary:
horgaszegyesulet.roszkenet.hu/node/2
golya.mme.hu/golyakamera/halaszstream
Black Stork in Estonian Forest:
www.unavitaverde.net/webcam-black-stork

• www.explore.org features several bird webcams, including owls, plus all sorts of other animals like bears and fish.

• Using a search engine, you can easily find other webcams on osprey, eagle, owl, and other bird nests.

It's an enormous task, but crews are working hard to rehabilitate the headwaters of the Clark Fork River by removing the poisonous slicken earth and replacing it with clean soil.

ORGANIZATIONS

DUNROVIN RANCH

In 2011, SuzAnne and Sterling Miller, owners of Dunrovin Ranch, bought a webcam and had it installed with help from the University of Montana when the power company relocated a big old nest from a dangerous power pole to its present location. Besides being the home of the webcam, this ranch on the shores of the Bitterroot River south of Missoula is a center for many outdoor activities, including horseback riding, river recreation, outdoor programs for children, and accommodations. In 2013, SuzAnne and Sterling added a night-vision camera so people around the world could enjoy the ospreys at any time of day or night. So far it's the only online webcam of this type. Already, the camera has shown that the ospreys don't necessarily sleep all night—they've been seen delivering fish after dark. The people who watch the ospreys can interact with one another by way of a chat feature on the ranch's www.DaysAtDunrovin.com website, as well as on the ranch's Facebook page. Many friendships have resulted. The viewers missed watching birds after they migrated, and many of them became so interested in the background scenes of ranch activities that they asked that the camera be kept on all year. This prompted Dunrovin to set up a second camera focused on the corral, where many of the ranch activities are centered. Because of the educational possibilities the ospreys and other ranch animals provide, SuzAnne has set up websites both for adults interested in what's going on (www.DaysatDunrovin.com) and for schools (www.SchoolDaysatDunrovin.com). The school site provides opportunities for schools around the world to cooperate in experiments and fun activities based in the ranch.

RAPTOR VIEW RESEARCH INSTITUTE

The mission of Raptor View Research Institute (www.raptorview.org) is to foster knowledge about raptors through research and education. Many raptors—ospreys, eagles, and hawks—live, breed, and hunt over a broad range of ecosystems. This makes them valuable indicators of ecosystem health. If the raptors are having a hard time surviving, there are probably serious problems with the ecosystem. The crash in populations of ospreys and other fish-eating birds that coincided with widespread DDT use is a perfect example.

In addition to providing transmitters to ospreys and helping in the banding and sampling work of the University of Montana team, Rob Domenech and his assistants tag golden eagles and other birds so they can be tracked. They also document the numbers of migrating raptors through traditional migration routes every spring and fall. This work provides valuable ongoing data for all raptor researchers and can help pinpoint problems in the ecosystems these powerful birds encounter as they migrate.

RAPTORS OF THE ROCKIES

Raptors of the Rockies (www.raptorsoftherockies.org), located in Florence, Montana, is home to about nineteen birds of fifteen different species whose injuries prohibit them from returning to the wild. The birds are kept in outdoor enclosures and fed their natural foods. Kate Davis takes some of her birds along on the eighty or so educational programs she gives each year to the public, schools, and other institutions.

CLARK FORK COALITION

Since 1985, the nonprofit Clark Fork Coalition (www.clarkfork.org), centered in Missoula, has worked toward protecting and restoring the beautiful Clark Fork River, the largest by volume in the state of Montana. The organization was a key player in bringing about the extraordinary cleanup now under way on the river. The coalition continues to work in the best interests of the river and the human communities and wild habitats it sustains.

Important and ongoing efforts include protecting clean, healthy streams, rivers, and lakes; restoring stream flows and habitats in damaged river corridors; running a riverside demonstration cattle ranch in an ecologically friendly manner; and inspiring people who live in the watershed to care for these waters for the long haul.

A golden eagle.

SOURCES AND ACKNOWLEDGMENTS

Working on this project has been a wonderful experience. The scientists, student helpers, and assistants were always cheerful and helpful. Erick, Heiko, and Rob have always responded quickly to my questions, even when they have been very busy with their work. They have been the most important source for information in the book, along with Poole's classic study, *Ospreys: A Natural and Unnatural History*. The various websites listed here have also provided important information. When I visited the Superfund workers unannounced, they were gracious and helpful. Katie Garcin, a scientist at the Montana Department of Environmental Quality, showed me around the site at the headwaters of the Clark Fork River, where workers are removing truckload after truckload of poisonous slickens, bringing in truckloads of uncontaminated soil, and planting thousands of native plants to revegetate the banks of the river. It's an amazing project. Ellen Crain of the Butte Silverbow Historical Society helped us find photos from the height of the Butte mining era. Chris Brick of the Clark Fork Coalition provided valuable information about the river's recovery.

• • •

The following people and institutions have been vital to the success of the osprey project:

Kate Davis and Raptors of the Rockies

Riverside Health Care Center, and especially director Tammy Talley, for support from the beginning and helping host all the camera feed and computer access

Northwestern Energy and especially Sam Milodragovich, for all they do for ospreys

Super thanks to Dave Taylor and Dave Taylor Roofing. We could not have done it without him!

University of Montana provided support in many ways; Division of Biological Sciences, Wildlife Biology Program, and Department of Geosciences

All the *many* ranchers and land owners who most graciously let us onto their land, and support our research

The State of Montana; the Natural Resources Damage Program is deeply committed to the restoration and reclamation of the Clark Fork River. They have supported our educational programs from the start (especially Carol Fox).

Clark Fork Watershed Education Program at Montana Tech in Butte. They have been partners from the beginning – especially Matt Vincent (now the mayor of Butte) and Rayelynn Connole.

Grant-Kohrs Ranch National Historic Site, especially Christine Ford

Karen Wagner and her family

EPILOGUE

Since this book was written, there have been two big changes in the program. The scientist Heiko Langner left Montana for a job managing a major laboratory at the King Abdullah University of Science and Technology in Saudi Arabia. And, sadly, Harriet's mate, Ozzie, died late in the 2014 season, from unknown causes. We all hope that Harriet finds a new mate as fine as Ozzie.

GLOSSARY

baling twine: Plastic rope used to hold hay bales together.

DDT: An insecticide widely used from the 1940s until 1972, when it was banned in the United States largely because of its effects on fish-eating birds.

egg tooth: A hard, sharp projection on the beak of a chick that helps it break through the shell of its egg. It falls off soon after the chick hatches.

heavy metals: Metallic elements that are toxic; most have a high atomic number.

methyl mercury: A dangerous chemical formed when mercury combines with what's called a methyl group.

oxidation: A process that occurs when a substance combines with oxygen to form a different chemical compound. More technically, oxidation is any chemical reaction in which an atom, molecule, or ion loses electrons.

raptor: A bird that hunts its prey, using its powerful talons and sharp beak. Eagles, hawks, falcons, ospreys, and owls are the most familiar raptors.

slickens: Deposits of poisonous mine wastes along the shores of polluted rivers where little or no life can survive.

Superfund: A federal program that handles cleanup of polluted areas.

top predator: A hunting animal at the top of the food chain.

talons: Curved, sharp claws, especially of a raptor.

INDEX

Page numbers in **bold** refer to photos and illustrations.

Abandoned Mine Lands program, 57
ARCO, 28, 29

bands and banding, 31, **32**, 34, **34**, 37, **37**, **43**
beak, 12, 18, **18**, 19, **49**, 50
Bird Banding Laboratory, 34
Bird's-Eye View Education Program, 12
bones, 13, **13**

Clark Fork Coalition, 74, 77
Clinger, Ashton, **60**, 60–61, **61**
coal, 58, **58**, 72
colonies, osprey, 21, **21**, 30
Confederated Salish and Kootenai Tribes, 29
Cooper, Harrison, 31, **31**, 37, 39, **71**
courtship behavior, 18

dangers to ospreys. *See also* pollution
    baling twine, 36, **36**, 37, **71**
    DDT, 25, 26, 77
    electrocution from power pole, 14, **24**
    mercury, 57–59, 69, 72
    predators, 19, 22, **24**, **25**
    toxins, 25, 26, 32, 34, 77
Davis, Kate, 15, 77
DDT, 25, 26, 77
diet. *See* fish
Dimauro, Marianna, 38, 39
diving, 13, 18
Domenech, Rob, 8
    background, 31
    banding birds, 31, 37, 77
    on future goals, 61, 69
    public education by, **71**
    radio transmitter work, 62, 64, 67, **67**, 77
    research, 31, **31**, 34
Dunrovin Ranch, 42, 48–51, **48–51**, 77

education, 8, 77
    conference, 70, **70–71**
    Riverside residents, 15
    visiting students, 10, 12–14, 16, **16**, 39
    webcams (*see* video cameras; webcam resources)
Egenhoff, Jay, **71**
eggs, 17, 18, **18**, 26, 44–45, **45**, 49. *See also* hatching
Eldermire, Charles, 71
evolution, 12

feathers and markings, 13, 17, **18**, 19, 50
fieldwork. *See* sample collection
fish
    and courtship behavior, 18
    danger to osprey (*see* food chain)
    osprey adaptations to hunt, 12
    osprey hunting technique, **12**, 13, **13**, **19**, 21, **21**
    sample collection, 60–61
fishing, recreational, 57–58, **58**
flight, 13, **17**, 18, 64
food chain, 25, 26, 34, 56–59
foot, toe, and talon, 12, **12**, **13**
Friends of the Osprey, 46

funding for research, 31, 46
future goals, 69, 70

glossary, 79
Greene, Erick
    background and interests, 21, 30, **30**
    public education by, **12**, 14, 16, **16**, 70, **71**
    research, 30, 60, 61
    video camera work, **6**, **7**, 8

habitat
    of ospreys, **40**
    restoration, 64, **76**, 77
hatching, **18**, 19, 49, **49**
heavy metals, 8, 26–29, 34, 35, 56–60, 69, 72
Hellgate Canyon. *See* Riverside Health Care Center nest
hunting. *See* fish

injured birds, reserve for, 77

Junda, James, 38, 39, **39**, 41, 71
juveniles, **11**, **17**, **19**
    feathers, 17, **18**, 19, 50
    fed by adults, 12, **18**, 19, **45**, 50, **50**
    hatching, **18**, 19, 49, **49**
    leaving the nest, 19, **19**, **45**, 51, **51**
    radio transmitters on, 62, **63**, 67, **67**

Kratina-Hathaway, Anicka, **31**, 71

laboratory work. *See* sample analysis
Langner, Heiko, **38**
    background and interests, 30, **30**
    camera maintenance by, **6**, **7**, 8
    laboratory work, 52, 54–55, **55**
    public education by, **71**
    research and fieldwork, 30, 34, **37**, 37–39, 61
legs, 13, **13**
Love Canal, New York, 28, **28**
Lund, Sherilee, **38**, 39

mass spectrometry, 54–55, **55**
McGrath, Ashley, 60
mercury, 57–59, 69, 72
Metcalf National Wildlife Refuge, **57**
methyl mercury, 57
migration, 7, **16**, 19, 20, 45, 69
Miles, Andrew, **31**, **46**
Miles, Gene, **31**, 46, **46**
Miller, Sterling, 49, 77
Miller, SuzAnne, 49, 77
Mills, Allison, **31**, 31, **71**
mining. *See also* heavy metals; Superfund
    contaminants in Clark Fork River, 8, **26**, 27, **27**, 29, 57–58, **76**
    history, 26, **26**, 59, **59**, 74
Missouri River, 60, **60**, 61
Montana
    Anaconda, **26**, 27, **27**
    Bitterroot River, **27**, 77
    Butte, 8, 26–27, **27**, 29, 34, 72
    Clark Fork River, 14, 28, **29**, **33**, 34 (*see also* under mining)
    Flint Creek, **27**, **56**, 57–58

Milltown Dam, 8, 26, 27, 29, **29**
    Warm Springs ponds, **27**, 28, **28**
Montana Fish, Wildlife and Parks, 28, 61
Montana Natural History Society, 39, **39**
Montana Osprey Project, 8, 30, 31, 46, **57**, 70, 74
MPG Ranch, 64, 69
Muñoz, Bill
    nest visits, 8, **9**, 34, 38, 64
    photographer, 7, 30
    radio transmitter work, 62, 64

nests
    construction, 8, 18, **18**, **47–49**, 48
    devices to discourage, 14
    difficult access to, 38, 39, **39**
    Dunrovin Ranch, 42, 48–51, **48–51**, 77
    empty, 8, **8**, **9**, **53**
    Hellgate Canyon (*see* Riverside Health Care Center nest)
    relocation, 15, **15**
    Riverside (*see* Riverside Health Care Center nest)
Northwestern Energy, 15
Northwest Power, 29
Nova Scotia, Cow Bay estuary, 21, **21**

Olson, Mary Torgrimson, 15, **15**
ospreys. *See also* dangers to ospreys
    as ecosystem barometers, 8, 24–25, 29, 32, 34, 77
    habitat, **11**, **21**, **40**
    population distribution, **16**
    statistics, 17
    as top predators, 24–25, 26
ospreys, individual
    Dilly, 49, **50**, 50–51, **51**
    Harriet, 24, 42, 48–51, **48–51**
    Hope, 49, 50
    Iris, 7, 14, 16, **16**, **23**, 42, **42–45**, 44–45, **69**
    Miles, 45, 46
    Ozzie, **24**, 42, 48–51, **48–51**
    Percy, 49, **49**, 50, **50**
    Rapunzel, **68**, 69
    Stanley, 7, 14, 16, 42, **42–45**, 44–45
    Taylor, 45, 46

Parker, Matt, 71
Patent, Dorothy Hinshaw
    airborne pollution experience, 72
    field experiences, 8, **9**, 34, 38–39, 41
Patent, Greg, 50, 51, 72
pollution
    acidic water, 26, 28
    airborne, 58, 59, 72, **72**, **73**
    DDT, 25, 26, 77
    heavy metals, 8, 26–29, 34, **35**, 56–60, 69, 72
    public education about, 12
    from railroad track runoff, 35, 61
    and Superfund, overview, 28, **28**
predators, 19, 22, **24**, **25**
publishing the results, 56–57, **57**, 70

radio transmitters, 62, **63**, 64, 67, **67**, **68**
Raptors of the Rockies, 15, 77
Raptor View Research Institute, 31, 62, 69, 74, 77

reproduction
    courtship behavior, 18
    decline due to DDT, 25, 77
    family size, 17, 49, **58**
    hatching, **18**, 19, 49, **49**
    incubation, 17, 18, **18**, 44–45, **45**, **49**, 49–50
    mates, 7, 18, **18**, 44–45, 48–49
resources, 74–75
Riverside Health Care Center nest
    empty nest, 8, **8**, **9**, **53**
    relocation, 15, **15**
    students' visit to, 10, 16, **16**
    video equipment, 7, **16**
    webcam on, 16, **16**, **23**, 42–45, **42–45**, **53**, **58**

sample analysis
    blood, 8, 52, **52**, **54**, 54–55, **55**, 61
    direct mercury analyzer, 61, **61**
    feather, 8, 61
    fish, 61, **61**
    goals of, 8, 61
    mass spectrometry, 54–55, **55**
    sediment, 61
sample collection
    adult ospreys, 8, 31, **31**, 34, **37**, 37–38, **38**, 61
    fish, 60–61
    juvenile ospreys, 38, **40**, 41, 61, 64, **66**
    sediment, 34, 41, **41**, 56, **60**, 61
satellite telemetry. *See* radio transmitters
Schrantz, Amanda Ormesher, **31**, 71
Shreading, Adam, **71**
skull, **12**
smelters, **26**, 27
Staats, Molly, 71
students, wildlife biology, 31, **31**, 46, 70, **70–71**
Superfund, 8, 27, **27**, 28, **28**, 34

tags. *See* bands
Taylor, Mike, 46
Taylor-Miles, Peggy, 45, 46, **46**
Times Beach, MO, 28
truck, roofing, **6**, 8, **9**, **34**, **36**, 64

University of Montana, 7, 30, 31, 52, 61, 75, 77

Van Ostrand, Roy, 8, 37, 39
video cameras
    aerial, remote-controlled, 39, **39**, 41
    Dunrovin Ranch nest, 48–51, **48–51**
    maintenance, **6**, **7**, 8
    motion-capture, 64, **64**
    Riverside (*see* Riverside Health Care Center nest)
    webcam resources, 77
vocalization, 18, 48, 70

Wagner, Karen, 15
Watershed Education Network, 12
webcam resources, 75
web sites, 12, 15, 28, 64, 74–75, 77
wings, 13, 17, 38

Young, Matt, 7, 31, **31**, 52, **54–55**